The Vision of the Nazarene

Cyril Scott

Illustrations by
David Anrias

WEISERBOOKS
Boston, MA/York Beach, ME

Published in 2002 by
Red Wheel/Weiser, LLC
York Beach, ME
With offices at:
368 Congress Street
Boston, MA 02210
www.redwheelweiser.com

Originally published in 1933 by George Routledge & Sons, Ltd., London.

Library of Congress Cataloging-in-Publication Data
Scott, Cyril, 1879–1970.
The vision of the Nazarene / Cyril Scott.
p. cm.
ISBN 1-57863-205-6 (pbk. : alk. paper)
1. Jesus Christ—Theosophical interpretations.
I. Title.
BT304.97 .S36 2000
232.9—dc21 00-040898

Printed in the United States of America
CCP

The paper used in this publication meets the minimum requirements of the American National Standard for Information Sciences—Permanence of Paper for Printed Library Materials Z39.48-1992(R1997).

The Vision of the Nazarene

CONTENTS

PART I

CONTENTS

PART II

INTRODUCTION

TO THE SECOND EDITION

As with older faiths, there are two aspects to the Christian religion, the exoteric as preached by the churches, and the esoteric, only studied by that small section of the public interested in mystical, theosophical and kindred subjects. Admittedly a large though decreasing number of people still accept the exoteric doctrine with its obsolete and confusing dogmas, yet with few exceptions it no longer satisfies the present-day intellectual or sophisticated type of mind. Thus, as the race becomes more and more mentally evolved, it is not extravagant to say that if the Christian religion is to survive, its esoteric truths will need to become more general knowledge, and cease to remain facts known only to students of the Arcane Science, and to those Initiates who constitute what is called The Hierarchy or the Great White Lodge.

Briefly, the esoteric truth, which includes

the doctrine of reincarnation, may be stated as follows: The Gospels are in part historical and even in greater part allegorical. They were written, so to say, round the life and teaching of the Initiate known to the world as Jesus of Nazareth, Who for a period was overshadowed by the much Higher Initiate, that Great Being, called in the West The Christ, and in the East, The Bodhisattva. He is also called the World Teacher, seeing that "to Him is committed the spiritual destinies of men". Nor is the exoteric reference to Him as "Saviour" inapt, in so far that in ages past He made the supreme sacrifice of incarnating on earth—having come from a planet far in advance of our own—so that He might further the evolution of this our world's very backward humanity. How and by what means remains a mystery save to Initiates; not because it *may* not be known, but simply because man still lacks the type of knowledge which would make it to him intelligible.

Some two thousand years ago, The Christ saw the need for founding a new religion more especially suited to the peoples of the occident, and it was for that purpose that He used Jesus of Nazareth as His willing Medium. Thus, the

Christian religion came into being. Jesus Himself, after accomplishing His mission in Palestine, reincarnated as Apollonius of Tyana, in which rebirth He took the fifth initiation, and so became one of the Masters of The Ancient Wisdom, as They are rightly called in view of Their high stage of evolution. In the Yogic philosophy He would be called a *jivanmukti*, namely one who had reached Liberation and need reincarnate no more. Yet being one of the Masters of Compassion, as They are also called, He renounced that disembodied form of Bliss-Consciousness so as to remain on our earth, the better to serve humanity and His own exalted Master, The Christ. At present He occupies a Syrian body, and much of His work consists in inspiring by telepathic means those souls in whom the spirit of service is developed and who are receptive to ideas for the betterment and upliftment of mankind.

Although the wishes and intentions of The Christ and of Jesus were that the Christian religion should be a guide and a stimulus to that right and fraternal conduct which in itself would bring about human betterment, how far short of realization Their wishes and intentions have fallen is something we know to our cost, and which Jesus Himself foresaw and foretold. He and The Christ divined only too truly that even the limited measure of free-will with which man is endowed would to a greater or lesser extent be misused.

And so it has happened throughout the whole of Christendom. Apart from the shameful fact that the Christian nations engaged in the two most destructive wars in history, the churches themselves (also throughout Christendom) have wrangled and fought with words, and what is worse, have at times used religion as a pretext for gaining political power. Indeed, love of power has been one of the most anomalous sins of the Roman Catholic Church, with her deplorable doctrine that only by submitting to her Authority could souls be saved.

Nor can it be denied that texts have been distorted and constructions put upon sayings attributed to Jesus which are entirely incompatible with the whole spirit of the Christ-Teachings. Further, in the early days of Christianity, religious frauds were perpetrated by copyists and translators of the scripts, thereby creating dogmas and discrepancies which theologians attempted to reconcile, but in later times were pounced upon by learned sceptics as evidence that the Christian religion itself was unfounded on fact.

All this being undeniable, long and arduous during the centuries has been the task of the great Founders of the Christian faith to save the noble "ark" which They built from shipwreck on the rocks of man's ineptitude. True, there are people who maintain that it *has* been shipwrecked, in other words, that it has proved a failure. But such people only judge it from its superficial effects, knowing little or nothing of those occult, spiritual Forces which have prevented the Dark Powers from achieving a complete and final triumph.

In any case, a part of Master Jesus' work has been and still is by means of the written word to counteract those baneful, doctrinal fallacies of the past, thereby seeking to inspire a greater spirit of tolerance, not only among the differing sects but also towards other religions. Indeed, to-day in these times of crisis when the need is ever more pressing to save man from the disastrous effects of wrong thinking and wrong action, He is using every available means, however modest and varied, to bring about that desideratum, the most important factor of which is Unity among all the peoples of the world.

The days have at least long since passed when any writer who contravened the dicta of The Church would have been burnt as a heretic. And yet even since the time when the following script was first penned, so many momentous things have happened, that it became expedient to add some new material and to make a few alterations in the original text. This Introduction has also been added for the especial consideration of those people who are no longer satisfied with agnosticism or with the exotericism presented by the Churches. Should such people be inclined to explore new fields of relevant knowledge, there is a prodigious amount of literature available.

II

Inspirational writing is older than Christendom itself, and practically all religious communities of whatever faith are familiar with it in one form or another. It is not to be confounded with automatic writing, the latter being a negative type in which the hand rather than the mind is used by some disembodied presence. As those who practise automatic writing are usually unaware of what they are setting down, their critical faculty is in abeyance, and they are therefore at the mercy of the entity who writes through them. With inspirational writing this is not the case; the transmitter is fully aware of all he sets down, and so is able to judge when the transmission is faulty.

To some people it may seem strange that in given circumstances both inspirational and scientific methods can be co-related; yet this is possible in so far that the veracity of inspirational writing can be authenticated by those who possess the necessary faculties. That the utterances in the script which herein follows were impressed on the writer by the Master Jesus, has been authenticated by two trained and independent investigators along the line of occult science.[1]

Of recent years an increasing number of people have become familiar with the term *astral body*, and some of them no longer dismiss as sheer delusion the possibility of functioning

[1] Both of these investigators are mentioned in the book, *The Initiate in the Dark Cycle* (Routledge).

in that *body* on other planes during sleep, whether the memory of the experience is afterwards registered by the physical brain or not. Hence, to such people, what the writer relates in the preliminary proem about his visit to the Master's garden in Syria, may not seem as irrational as it would have done in the days when agnosticism was regarded as an aspect of progressiveness.

As for the actual text, in some instances, notably in Part II, the services of a fellow pupil with occult knowledge and powers greater than those of the writer, were called upon—services which are most gratefully acknowledged.

To be explicit, it is difficult even for a Master to impress the mind of His medium relative to matters with which that medium is unfamiliar. Indeed, the medium's mind may be likened to a piano: if some of its notes are missing, the musician however gifted will be considerably hampered by the limitations imposed.

With regard to the stylized language of the script, apart from the fact that the Master has certain characteristics of speech—was He not an adept at poetical expression when He trod the earth of Palestine?—the somewhat Biblical language is particularly suited to rhetorical utterance.

Finally, spiritual pride with its self-assertiveness being one of the dangers which beset the neophyte on the occult or mystical Path, the writer desires as far as may be still possible to remain anonymous.

PART I

Teacher of Angels and Men

THE PARABLE OF THE ROPE AND THE RIVER

Prolonged and deep had been my meditation, so deep that my soul had left my body.

And I was transported to a garden in a country far away from my dwelling-place. Yet was that garden familiar to me, and the faces of some of those who walked therein as they conversed lovingly together, for oftentimes had I been in that garden before. And I stood beneath the spreading branches of a great cedar-tree, and watched, and waited, knowing that I had come to this sanctified place for a purpose. And presently towards me along one of the paths came that Great One Whom I had always desired to serve. And as He approached, I was dazzled by the resplendence of His aureole, which was of surpassingly beautiful colours suffused with gold.

And He embraced me, and said: "My son,

wouldst thou serve me again as thou didst serve me in the past?"[1]

And I answered: "Gladly will I do so, if only I may know in what way it lies in my power?"

And He smiled and said:

I will tell thee a parable. Know that once there were two countries, and the one was a land flowing with milk and honey, and the other an arid region, full of strife and unrest, so that the one was called the Land of Bliss and the other was called the Land of Woe. But between these two countries was a swift, wide and dangerous river, and many who sought to cross that river lost their lives in the attempt.

And then one day there came a man who, because of his love for the people, said: "Lo, I will endeavour to place a rope from one bank to the other, and even if I lose my life in the attempt, what matter, for others will henceforward be able to cling to the rope and so cross the river in safety."

So saying, that man proceeded to carry out his design; and having procured a rope, he

[1] The writer had an incarnation as an early Christian mystic, in which he contacted and was able to render service to the Master Jesus.

fixed one end to a tree, and made a noose at the other, and plunged into the current to battle with the waves.

But while he was battling, some hunters who had come to the bank shot at him with their arrows and mortally wounded him; for amidst the spray and the splash of the waters they deemed him to be some animal and not a man at all.

Nevertheless, with a last and great effort, he managed to throw the noose of his rope round the stump of a tree, ere he sank beneath the waves; and thus had he carried out his design, though he lost his life because of those hunters and their lack of discernment.

Now when the people saw what had happened, they began to worship him as a hero, saying he died to save us, and so is he worthy of our adulation and love.

And yet although they worshipped him, only a very few attempted to cross the river, for they said within themselves: "Even though the rope is there and we cannot drown if we cling thereto, yet are the waters cold, and the river is wide, and the trouble of crossing is very great."

And so in the course of time, the rope was

almost forgotten; moreover, through disuse it had become covered with weeds and entangled in the fallen branches of old trees, so that hardly did it look like a rope at all.

But the worship of that hero continued nevertheless; and monuments were erected to his memory, and people sang songs of adulation to him and prayed to him because of his great love for them.

And then as a second and third and fourth generation of men came into being, there arose wiseacres and orators and men of learning; and of the hero they preached, and how he had died to save others; but of the rope across the river they never spoke, for now it had been forgotten altogether.

And so great a confusion arose by reason of their arguments and oratory and teachings, that finally many superstitions came to be, both among themselves and among their hearers; and only the very few were able to discern between folly and truth.

And much discord was sown amongst them, so that they quarrelled and fought; and those few who were able to discern the truth, they persecuted and reviled, so that the country called the Land of Woe became more stricken with sorrow and unrest than already it was.

And then at last a body of orators arose, and they cried: "Why this strife? All that is needful is to worship this hero as a god, and to believe that he died to save others, and lo! when we ourselves die we shall go to the country called the Land of Bliss without any trouble at all. For although our bodies cannot float across the river while we are alive, our souls will float across it when we are dead. Moreover, so great were his love and power and heroism, that all we ask of his Spirit he will surely do, if we but shower enough love upon him in return."

Then when the populace heard this, they were overcome with exceeding joy, and heaped honours upon those orators, saying: "Great is their wisdom, for they have shown us an easy way. Simple indeed is it to worship and to pray and to ask our hero to save us when we die; so now let us eat, drink and be merry and make the best of our sojourn in our Land of Woe."

But meanwhile the spirit of that hero looked upon his brothers with sadness in his eyes as he listened to their prayers and petitions. And into their ears he whispered:

"My children, ye do err, for verily I *lived* to save you, and my death was but an incident of my attempt, and can never be the cause of your salvation.

"Alas that ye should have forgotten the rope which I placed across the River between the Lands of Woe and Bliss, for to that end did I come and to no other.

"And although because of my love for you, my spirit is close to you and would fain comfort and cheer you in your adversities, yet carry you across the River I cannot, however much ye may pray and implore."

But although that hero spoke to them thus, yet too loud did they utter their prayers and petitions to hear the still small voice of his spirit, so did they remain in the Land of Woe.

And the Radiant One said, as He smiled:

And now that is the end of my parable, and its name is superstition.

And I said:

Master! Have I understood Thy parable aright; and do I divine correctly its meaning? For those who come to regard the non-essential as the essential and to act accordingly, verily are they tainted with superstition.

And He answered:

My beloved, thou hast spoken truth. Moreover, know that as the Enlightened One[1] said very long ago, "Each one must carry out his own salvation."

Nevertheless, thou canst help thy brethren, and in helping them canst serve me. For know that the greatest and best of all help is that which inspires man to help himself.

And I answered Him:

O Master, to this end didst Thou come, but Man has failed to understand?

And He answered:

Again hast thou spoken truth; for verily I have been misunderstood, ay, from the very first I have been misunderstood, and my Mission also, which was to show humanity the way.

And although mighty fanes have been dedicated to me and my name is engraven in countless books, and that which men think to be my likeness is in manifold places, even so, those very nations who profess to believe in me have not tried my way.

And I have been misrepresented even by my own chroniclers, and portrayed as addicted to unrighteous anger and conceit and gross self-aggrandizement, and other unseemly things.

[1] Buddha.

Yet in spite of ascribing to me these inordinations have my followers wanted to exalt me to the status of Deity, and have quarrelled over the manner in which I should be worshipped.

Worship! Did I ever ask for worship or adulation and for a deluge of flatteries to be poured into mine ears?

Verily, I came to point the way to Peace and fraternity through the education of the heart and the will to love all beings.

And to that end I gave to my disciples and to the world at large, many precepts and sayings. But despite my warnings, man hath misinterpreted those sayings, and even made them a plea for all manner of evil things—of hatred and warfare and uncharitableness and bigotry, or at best, not wishing to follow them, hath called them unpractical and the dreams of a visionary.

Thus have my devotees illogically deemed me to be "the only begotten Son of God" and a representative of God on earth, and at the same time have so greatly doubted His Wisdom as to assume that He would propound Divine Laws and rules of conduct impossible of carrying out!

Basic, spiritual Truths did I reveal to man for his right guidance, so that security and peace should be his on earth; ay, more than that, for, because of my love for him, I wished him to have Life and have it more abundantly, as I did say erewhile; meaning thereby that One Life which is Pure Being, Intelligence and Bliss—and is ultimately for all.

But, alas for my Mission, and, alas, for my burning hopes. And, alas, for the nations, who, although professing to love me, have sought not to keep my commandments, and so brought about their own undoing.

Belief in me yet disbelief in my precepts!—a strange and paradoxical belief is that indeed.

And so, my son, because men have misunderstood me and the purport of my Mission, do I seek, in these times of danger and crises and tribulations, to bring back many things to remembrance.

And thus saying, the Radiant One took me by the hand, and led me away to the cities, in the midst of which we wandered, invisible to men.

OF PRIESTS AND DIGNITARIES

And He took me first to a city where there was a large cathedral. And He said, with a smile in which there was a touch of rue:

Lo, in this city are those who call themselves my ministers, and who preach the "good tidings" and the "Gospel of Love". Yet although many among them are noble souls with a compassionate regard for their fellows and a steadfast devotion to *me*, there are others who are my ministers only in name, and in whose hearts dwelleth a love of power and of adulation rather than a love of God.

And though they proclaim the "glad tidings" with their lips, often do their faces belie their words, which some of them utter in lugubrious accents, and others, tonelessly, as if indifferent to their meaning.

And some of these my ministers in name, walk with great pride and an air of self-righteousness, deeming themselves to possess the only key to Truth, even though I taught my disciples to practise humility, saying, *blessed are the humble in spirit*; since only the humble of mind and spirit are receptive to enlightenment.

Alas, that they should shut the door to Knowledge by reason of their watertight convictions, and shut their ears to my voice which fain would whisper to them a little more of Truth. . . . But who listens to gentle voices who deemeth to know all himself?

And wherefore, my son, do my proclaimers of glad tidings clothe themselves in garments of mourning? Rather would I wish to see them clad in less sombre apparel.

Yet there are others who dress in scarlet and fine linen as a mark of their spiritual status; and this, even though by my example I desired to teach unostentation.

But think not that I deprecate all grandeur and pomp and ceremony when employed for righteous ends and in the right spirit, for they have their place in the Divine Purpose. Gloom and gloominess do I deprecate, and the assumption on the part of some of my misguided followers that colour and beauty are unrighteous and ungodly and pertaining to "the Devil".

Is it not written in my Gospels: *The*

Kingdom of God is within you—yet think these gloomy ones that the kingdom of God is misery and ugliness instead of Joy?

Although my words were unequivocal, too little have my ministers proclaimed the joyful immanence of God, so that knowing it man should realize his inherent divinity.

Verily, right thought giveth life and health, and giveth it more abundantly, and the immanence of God is a right thought. But too much have my ministers chosen to stress only His transcendence, thus believing themselves to be His intermediaries.

As leaders of prayer and performers of uplifting ceremonies, and as ministers to the sick and sorrowing do I bless my priests.

OF DOGMAS

Then the Shining One led me into a church, in which an aged man with great vehemence was exhorting his listeners to believe in the Immaculate Conception and other dogmas.

And the Master smiled with a touch of amusement as He said:

Verily a strange opinion hath that agèd man of me, and much oratory and force doth he expend upon his listeners, charging them to believe what is of no importance at all.

For wrongly doth he think that wrathful would I become did my followers deem me to have been conceived like all other men born of woman.

O my son, strangely inconsistent are men, for they have identified me with the God of Love, and worship me thus with their lips, yet think that Love can care one whit how they imagine I was conceived.

Yet, alas, if I look into their hearts, I see that they are secretly glad of a pretext for wrangling among themselves, and are glad to find, as they think, an easy way to salvation.

For truly it is easier to profess belief in the difficult of imagination than to love their enemies and do good to those who bear them a grudge. Verily did I declare that there was only one prerequisite to salvation, and that was to "love God and thy neighbour as thyself".

An offence to the intelligence of Man are dogmas, and never were they of my own creating, for truly do they cramp the heart and the mind and engender a plea for separateness instead of unity.

But, alas that my ministers should have lost the key to my allegories, and so should preach folly, distorting my teachings, and filling the minds of my devotees with unessentials and superstitions, thus bringing my philosophy into disrepute.

For know that much that I said of myself did I mean to apply to all, and not to me alone. Nevertheless, through failure to understand the mystic significance of many of my utterances, was the dogma created that I was "the only begotten Son of God",[1] whereas mystically understood, ye are all sons of God

[1] It is now more or less admitted by savants that this was a fragment of glossary which should not have been incorporated in the text.

—ay, of the Great White Spirit, the Light of the world, in Whom we live and move and have our being.

Moreover, this would I say unto all those who love me yet are perplexed because of my teachings: From more than one angle was I wont to speak, that each man should receive those truths best adapted to his mental or emotional needs and the path most suited for him to tread.

Thus, at times did I speak from the angle of dualism and at times from the angle of monism; the one not basically conflicting with the other when finally understood.

Yet, lacking in that understanding, did theologians and text-twisters and power-loving men interpret my scriptures according to the letter instead of to the spirit, and literalize did they the language of poetry and metaphor, so that discrepancies and absurdities and dogmas were the result.

And now listen to a parable: once there suddenly appeared in a place where there dwelt none but lepers, a physician, and in his hand was a phial, and in that phial was a cure for all ills.

And he said to those lepers: Hearken well unto my words, for he who would be cured by the elixir contained in this phial must follow my instructions and retain them in his mind; seeing that although I may leave the elixir with you, yet I may not remain myself.

And then he proceeded to instruct them how the treatment should be effected: and having done this, he handed the phial to one of the lepers, and said: Do thou take charge of this, suffering each one of thy comrades to take the prescribed dose. So saying, that physician vanished.

And no sooner had he departed, than those lepers began to argue among themselves, not only as to who he might be, but also as to the manner in which he had come and in which he had gone.

And so intense was their argumentation and so vehement, that all his instructions escaped their minds, never to be recovered.

Thus, although the precious phial remained in their midst, not one of them knew how to apply its contents, so that it was utterly useless, and like a ship-wrecked treasure hidden beneath the sea.

And now, that is the end of my parable, and dear to me is he who can understand and pay heed to its meaning.

OF SECTS AND SECTARIANS

And the Radiant One led me unto another church where a white-robed priest exhorted his listeners to provide money for the conversion of the heathen.

And again the Master smiled as He said:

O my disciple, did I ever say, Lo! there is but one belief and one religion that is right, and all others, verily they are wrong? Yet because I said to my disciples: *Go ye unto all the world and preach the good tidings,* the unreflecting have misinterpreted my words and made of them a plea for wasteful and foolish deeds.

For verily by this did I mean that each one should spread abroad my gospel of peace, bringing comfort and enlightenment to his fellows, because of Love and kindness of heart —but not that man should sow seeds of dissension and strife, arrogant in the conviction that he alone is right and all others are wrong.

Truly God is One, but by many names may He be called by His devotees: yet alas do my followers distress themselves much because of those many names.

But to them would I say: "Ere ye condemn the religion of another, see to it first that ye understand that religion, and see to it also that ye understand your own religion: for in essence all are the same."

O my disciple, not a matter of belief is conversion, but a matter of the heart; and much do the unreflecting seek to convert those who are already converted, and their desire to convert all too often arises from lack of humility.

But did I not say erewhile: *I came not to destroy the law and the prophets, but to fulfil them;* nevertheless, my followers seek to discountenance those older religions in spite of my words—and this, because they have lost the understanding of the law and the prophets.

Verily all religions are One, and he who worships the Father worships Brahman, and he who worships Brahman worships Tao, for all these are but the various names for Love—Existence—and Bliss Absolute, which in truth, are God.

Unity did I preach, for what greater unity could there be than to *love thy neighbour as thyself?* And verily he is thyself, for all Life is one.

And hence, sympathy and understanding did I preach—feeling *with* and understanding *with*; for these truly are the children of Love.

But in spite of my saying: *By this shall all men know that ye are my disciples, if ye have love one to another*, yet have my followers been guilty of religious intolerance and have worked not together in unity and fellowship, but in separate communities, one reviling the other.

And now learn, O my belovèd, Truth is infinite although it be One, and not in this or that sect, or in this or that book is *all* Truth contained; nevertheless, to the selfless of heart shall Truth be revealed.

OF IDOLATRY

And the Shining One led me into a far land, and into a little village where a great statue of the Buddha was, and before which was a devotee in an attitude of devotion.

And the Holy One said:

My beloved, when thou dost feel love and gratitude towards one of thy fellows, thou dost place his likeness before thee, and dost love to gaze thereon, and no one says thee nay.

Yet because this my brother doth prostrate himself out of love and gratitude before the likeness of Him Who showed the way to peace, verily do some of my followers condemn him, saying he worships idols and is a heathen and an idolator.

It were expedient ere one condemns, to strive to understand; and to this end did I say long ago, *Judge not that ye be not judged,* for in the eyes of God, this my brother is not an idolator.

Too prone are the non-understanding to imagine this devotee doth worship an image of stone, yet truly doth he worship that Being of which this image is but a symbol, as the likeness of any loved one is but a symbol of that loved one.

Lo, there are those who prostrate themselves before an image of me, yet only the intolerant denounce them as idolators.

Ah, worse idols there are even than images of stone, and more harmful; and the foolish worship these, laying them up as treasures for themselves upon earth.

Ay, riches do they worship, and pleasure and fame and name, and other things which all too soon corrupt in themselves, and also corrupt the hearts of those who unto them are attached.

Yet fain would these idolators break the images of those my loved ones who are of another faith, though their own idols of wealth and power they would strive with all their strength to keep intact.

And some of them would also break the likenesses of me, saying in their lack of understanding: "In our Religion idolatory shall not be, away with this degradation!"

But know, O my belovèd, that even they who worship neither wealth nor images—even they may be idolators; for verily he who exalts the Letter and the symbol of the Scripture in place of the spirit and the import, he too must be accounted an idolator before the Lord.

And further would I say, even those who worship God as a person have something of the spirit of idolatry in their hearts; for of the Absolute and Infinite would they make the relative.

Likewise, too often did my chroniclers confound me, the person, with the Way and the Divine Essence that I came to reveal.

Is it meet that any man should say of himself, *I am the Way, the Truth, and the Light?* And so did I tell my disciples: *The words that I say unto you I speak not from myself, but the Father abiding in me doeth His works.* Never for worship did I ask: nay, I rebuked him who called me good, saying there is One alone Who is good, and that is God—yet have many of my followers failed to heed that rebuke.

If for discipline I asked love, not for my sake was it, but alone for theirs: for truly is Love the highest nourishment for the soul of him who loves.

And now, O my brother, teach unto thy fellows that in all men is the Father, and for all men is God-Consciousness who make themselves One with the Father: and to be One with the Father is to be one with all beings, and to realize the Essence of Existence and Knowledge and Bliss Absolute.

Yet know that he who deems to conceive of God in the plenitude of His Nature is guilty of presumption, for it is as impossible for a man to conceive of God, as for the ant on its anthill to conceive of man. Nevertheless did I call God "The Father": yet is He more than the Father; and God is Love, yet is He more than Love—nay, God is all that it is possible to conceive of, yet is He more than is possible to conceive of.

And so saying the Master bathed that devotee of the Buddha with His radiance, so that that devotee deemed that radiance came from the Buddha Himself, and rejoiced exceedingly. And the Radiant One smiled as He led me back to His own garden.

OF FAITH, TESTIMONY AND UNDERSTANDING

And the Master said:

Once did one of my converts say: *Prove all things, hold fast to that which is good;* yet there are those calling themselves my followers who pronounce it a wickedness to seek to *prove* immortality. "Believe and have faith," they say, "and the more purblind that faith, the more meritorious, for did not the Master say, *Blessèd is he who believeth though he hath not seen?*"

Thus do they convict me of exalting stupidity as almost the highest of virtues. Ay, because I said in effect: *Blessèd are the little children*, they deemed me to have said "Blessèd is ignorance." Yet did I mean, blessèd are the unprejudiced and the humble in knowledge.

Right faith is there and wrong faith; and the former is based upon right discernment, but the latter is like a house built upon shifting sands.

Would those who are sick go to a physician

except he could convince them of his power to heal? Yet having convinced them, truly hath he given them understanding, and hence, faith, born of understanding.

Or again; would those go to a physician who had never healed others? Verily they go because those others have borne testimony, and hence is their faith the outcome of that testimony, and thus also based on a measure of understanding.

A mighty power is right faith, and to some who came to me erewhile did I say, *Thy faith hath made thee whole;* but no good works could I do among those who lacked understanding altogether, for unbelief was an obstacle in my path.

O my disciple, know that he who understands and has sufficient faith in my teachings to follow them, he alone hath faith in me.

But alas, too much in my name and too little in my teachings have the peoples had faith; and so did I fail to save them from terrible tribulations.

OF PRAYER AND WORSHIP

And the Radiant One said:

With strong words did I of old wage war against hypocrisy, but many of those who pray to me even in these latter days are hypocrites unbeknown to themselves.

Wise is he who knows how to pray and for what to pray, lest his lips ask for one thing and his heart desire another.

Lo! hypocrites are they who pray unto the Father: *Thy Kingdom come on earth*—the Kingdom of Love and Harmony—yet having hatred and discord in their hearts, wilfully frustrate the advent of that very thing for which they pray.

Nevertheless, Divine Service do they call their worshipping. But where, alas, may be found the service, and where the divinity?

To my disciples I said: *When ye pray, enter into your most quiet and secret chamber*—ay, and now I add, *even the secret chamber of your hearts*—for never did I uphold ostentation and a display of prayerfulness.

Dear to me is he who sings the name of God continually in his own heart, wheresoever he be, for verily the name of God is Love, and he who continually feels Love is the true worshipper.

Ay, I said erewhile, the time shall come when man shall worship God in Spirit and in Truth, for God is Spirit and Truth; and this I prophesied because I foresaw the day when man shall have attained to greater enlightenment.

Nevertheless, I also said: *Wherever two or three are gathered together in my Name, there am I in the midst of them.* But again many have misinterpreted the meaning of my Name.

For know that those who are gathered together in harmony, peace and love, and who call to me in the spirit of Service, they verily are gathered together in my Name, and to them I come, because like attracts like.

But those who are gathered together to perform ceremonies with errant minds and hearts yearning for worldly things, to them do I not come, for their wandering thoughts never reach me at all.

And yet, think not that I am averse to all ceremonies even though I raised my voice against vain repetitions; for know that ritual and ceremonies are as the crutches to the lame of spirit, to be discarded when man has become whole in spirit.

Lo, nowadays many do scoff at these crutches of the halt and feeble. And their scoffing is born of intolerance; yet in ritual devoutly performed there is my Power and my Love.

And in some repetitions also there is my Power, but in others there is only foolishness and even harmfulness; for man, by reason of his materialism, has lost the Golden Key to the right use of my Ritual and my Words of Power.

And now, would I say; he who prays with true sincerity for the happiness of others shall obtain happiness himself, and he who prays for the enlightenment of others shall obtain enlightenment himself; for so doth he open the door to that Pure Consciousness which is Unity and Joy.

OF THE HOLY SACRAMENT

And we came to a church in which the Holy Sacrament was being administered.

And the Master said:

Of rites and ceremonies have I spoken, and their usefulness to those who stand in need thereof. And yet not all rites performed in my name originated with me; from older religions have some of them been taken.

Hark to the words which that priest doth now enunciate, believing them to have first been spoken by me to my disciples at the last supper we partook together. Nevertheless they were derived from a more ancient Creed, as delvers into the Past have since discovered.

Verily no more have these words aught to do with my body and blood than with the body and blood of him who repeateth them. Only a symbolic significance have those words; but, knowing it not, have learned unbelievers made them one more pretext to call my religion a fraud and a fabrication.

But this would I ask; what proof have they

that I did not teach my disciples the ancient rite, so that it might be enacted in memory of me?

Ah, a mystery hath that rite been even to my followers, yea so deep a mystery that they must needs invent the doctrine of Substantiation in their endeavour to explain it, thereby persuading themselves that one mystery could be solved by creating an even greater one.

A mystery forsooth it may be, but not to the clear-visioned and to the initiated. For verily the rite if correctly performed doth invoke a great Deva[1] whose Radiance, streaming forth on to all participants, uplifteth their hearts and purifieth their emotions, according to their capacity and willingness to receive.

But the day of understanding is not yet; for only when Man hath acquired the faculty to see those subtler things which as yet are hidden, will the truth anent this invocative ceremony be proven and known.

[1] An Angel, in Christian terminology.

OF THE ORTHODOX AND THE UNORTHODOX

And the Radiant One said:

Lo, even in these days of vaunted enlightenment there are still many who are proud of their orthodoxy, but there are many more who are proud of their unorthodoxy, saying within themselves, "We are more emancipated than our fellows."

Thus they have become puffed-up with self-importance and spiritual pride, little realizing that they are as hard and unyielding in their unorthodoxy as those very orthodox ones whom they disparage.

So they are deaf to the whisperings of my voice in the depths of their souls, for verily I would say to them: "Not at the belief, but at the heart do I look, and the pure of heart, be they ever so orthodox in belief, are dearer to me than the proud of spirit."

Fain would I warn thee against the insidious dogmatism of new sects and new fraternities, for he who prides himself on his freedom from dogmatism may already have become dogmatic in his own heart.

Behold, there are some who don new religions as they don new garments, yet do their characters remain the same none the less.

Often have I heard it said: "Freedom of thought and differing opinions do we encourage in our fraternity"; but woe unto him who takes them at their word; for his differing opinions are greeted by antagonism and disapproving looks!

Narrowness of mind was never dear to me, and conversely breadth of mind did I ever love; yet alas, many who embrace a broader religion do not remember to leave their narrow-mindedness at home.

And self-honesty and the absence of self-deluding did I also love, but some there are who embrace new sects not for the sake of what is taught, but for the sake of those who teach.

Love, thankfulness and reverence towards leaders and teachers are good and beautiful, but unwise and idolatrous is he who adulates and worships them, for easily may he be allured along the path to false knowledge.

He who worships a person, inwardly exalts

that person into a God, and hence believes that every word that proceedeth from his mouth must perforce be true.

Nay, worship of persons—how often doth it not engender slothfulness of mind and an all too ready acquiescence? Yet shall man use his reason and his intuition to separate the tares of false beliefs from the wheat of Truth.

Lo, because man likewise exalted me into a God were his eyes blinded and his reason glamoured and stunned, so that even the mistakes and contradictions discrepancies of my chroniclers he endowed with verisimilitude.

And learned men argued, and councils were held and innumerable books were written to justify those mistakes, and to prove in seeming that they were not mistakes at all, but the mysteries of God and His inspired word.

And those more enlightened ones who rejected the fruits of these argumentations and saw with the eyes of Truth were denounced as heretics and many of them suffered martyrdom at the stake.

Nevertheless, because I foresaw those evil happenings, and how my sayings would be distorted and perverted and made a plea for cruelty and torment and bloodshed, I warned my disciples and those who came after them. For I said: *Agree with thine adversary quickly while thou art with him in the way, lest haply the adversary deliver thee to the judge, and the judge deliver thee to the officer and thou be cast into prison. Yet did I utter my warning in vain.*

Nay, those courageous martyrs failed either to apply my words to their own needs or else comprehended them not, or again had no desire to comprehend them; for even some kinds of martyrdom are inspired by an insidious form of vanity.

Courage of mind and courage of body, these are qualities worthy of praise; but he who would sacrifice his body in a wasteful cause is possessed of an unwise courage.

Some good but also some harm have martyrs wrought; for many have only served as instruments to endow the unimportant with an unwarranted importance.

Strange though it may seem to many of my devotees, yet those who suffered death in the cause of Science or Freedom of thought achieved greater results than many of those who suffered death in the cause of religion.

Ay, merely to bolster-up or negate some

theological conclusion have many martyrs died, deeming the while that they died to please me; yet ever more dear to me was the living body of one who served his fellows than a dead body laid beneath the soil.

But again have I been misunderstood and the very nature of my Love debased in the eyes of men; since only an infatuated woman rejoices to hear that one whom she loves is ready to die for her sake.

Lo, my watchword is: "Live and serve"; and if ye have a little more of knowledge than your fellows, be not proud, for it is but as one drop in the ocean of infinite knowledge which is of God.

OF SINNERS AND THE SAVING OF SINNERS

And the Master said:

Alas for those who seek only to save themselves; for he who would save himself must strive to save others, because that very striving is the door which leads to salvation.

Truly, blessed to me is the figure who stands with one hand stretched high to receive, and the other hand stretched out to give; for God gives to those who give unto others.

And yet only the wise and joyful ones know *how* to give, for the foolish have nothing to offer except sad looks and lugubrious words, and a nebulous far-away reward.

"Believe as we do," they say, "and try to be like the 'Man of Sorrows,' and thy reward shall be the entrance into a far-away place of continual worship, when thou art dead." But they do not add: "We ourselves have never seen that place"; and they forget that erewhile I said the Kingdom of Heaven is *within* and *around* you.

O my wise ones, what manner of a physician is he who says to his patient: "My medicine will cure thee some day very far hence?" For the skilled physician is he who can cure his patients here and now or in the near future.

But alas, much of the desire to "save" others is based upon vanity and not upon Love: for it arises not from the selfless wish that others may attain spiritual joy, but that those who seek to save them may take credit to themselves.

Countless times, through lack of understanding, have my followers besought God, saying: "Have mercy upon us, miserable sinners." Yet I say unto thee, he who repeatedly calls himself a miserable sinner blasphemes in the depths of his ignorance. For man is potentially divine and his spirit was made perfect in the image of God and is one with God.

Ay, this doctrine did I teach long ago when I said: *I and my Father are One.* Yet because of nescience, doubters called me a braggart and my followers exalted me as an exception to the Divine rule.

Yet what I said once I say again, and thus

do I bid men to pray: "Because Thou and I are one, O Father, help me to manifest in my mind and body more of Thy Perfection, that I may become what in reality I am—the Essence of Love and Bliss."

OF GOVERNMENTS AND RULERS

And we passed by an imposing edifice, in which the Affairs of State were being enacted.

And the Master said:

Ah, my brother, what greater delusion than the belief that the world at large can be governed by men deficient in uprightness, whose striving it is to outwit their fellows, and who scorn not to lie and cheat and deceive the multitudes when it suiteth their purpose.

Order and crookedness—these, forsooth, are incompatibles; so how can Rulers with crooked minds and morals and conscience create and preserve order in a disordered world?

Verily, respect for those who govern is a prerequisite to sound government, for people are more ready to obey those whom they revere and who set to all a noble example. But who, I ask, doth respect liars and cheats and promise-breakers and excuse-finders? Nay, often are such men merely targets for ridicule or contempt.

Adepts of plausibility are they and the

craft of decrying their opponents, but little there is of altruism in their hearts. Nevertheless, a few altruists I see among them, who strive to make their voices heard, only to be shouted down alas, as unpractical dreamers, visionaries and inexpert diplomats.

In the world of affairs, two kinds of diplomats there are, as thou knowest well; the one, clever at constructing ambiguous phrases, and the other, skilled in the gentle art of smoothing out rough places. Ah, would that to-day there were more of the latter type to throw oil on the billows of man's contentiousness. Yet this do I say; there *will* be when the evil age of Power-Politics hath passed away.

Power-Politics and Power-Politicians!, in wellnigh all lands do they abound to a lesser or greater degree, and where they abound to the fullest degree terrible torments have my loved-ones been doomed to suffer.

To command respect through fear—such is the way of power-loving tyrants. Ay, through fear, because they themselves are afraid.

Afraid they are of the consequences of their transgressions, forever apprehensive lest the peoples they have deceived and oppressed should rise up and tear them asunder.

And not alone of the masses are they afraid, but of each other, as also of philosophers and poets and playwrights and story-tellers—and above all, of religion. Too much did I speak of freedom, so think they, therefore do they hate and fear my teachings.

Rulers they may be, yet when I look into their hearts I see that their love of ruling is seldom for the sake and welfare of the multitudes, but so that *they* might enjoy the powers and privileges of rulership; though they pretend 'tis for the good of The State.

Worship of The State! Lo, such is the newest subtlest and most useful form of idolatry, created and exploited to cover an abundance of sins; and one of them is the degrading of Service.

Willing service to The State for the welfare of the masses, *that*, forsooth, is a beautiful thing ennobling to the soul. But wherein lies the merit of service under compulsion; do not straight thinkers who call things by their true names denounce it as slavery in a new guise? Moreover, he who serves not willingly and joyously most often serves badly, and maybe with revengefulness smouldering in his heart.

Not enforced service, but the *spirit* of service did I account a blessed thing; therefore, by way of setting an example, I washed the feet of my disciples, and enjoined them to do a like service unto each other. Symbolic was my act of the blessedness of Service.

The spirit of service!—joyous are they who have it in their hearts, and blessèd the day when Service-Politics shall supplant Power-Politics, and the nations shall serve each other according to their capacities, irrespective of their differing ideologies.

Ask me not to prophesy as to Time: for how soon or how long delayed its dawning must depend on man himself. Only this will I say: the dark ages of Power-Politics are already numbered. For Power without Love is an evil thing, and destined to destroy itself in the end.

Verily, no mere sentiment is Love, as the scoffers delight to maintain. Ay, Love is the Force which upholds and keeps the Universe together.[1] And even if man with his destruc-

[1] Viz. Love is a scientific fact, and will one day be recognized as such.

tive follies should shatter his world-habitation, he cannot destroy those worlds which are indestructible,[1] nor can he destroy his own soul.

[1] I.e. the higher Planes of consciousness.

OF THE REAL CHARITY

And the Master led me back towards mine own country. And as we wandered through a town we saw a man who carelessly tossed a coin to a beggar.

And the Radiant One said:

O my disciple, much dost thou hear speak of charity in the world, and much giving is there of alms; yet unless man gives a portion of himself therewith does he give but little.

Charity is of the heart more than of the hand, and very near to me are those who give Love, yet are unconscious of the giving.

Know that he who takes a sinner to his own heart and to his own hearth, regardless of what others say, and does this to try to teach him wisdom, gives more than he who bestows gifts of money on charitable institutions.

And know also that he who thinks well of a man when others think evil, performs an act of charity in his own heart.

An attitude of the mind is charity, and very charitable is he in whose heart dwells the spirit of service, and in whom dwells eternal forgiveness.

For the charitable one is he who forgives even before there is aught to forgive; and so is he immune to all wrongs.

Ay, charitable is he who thinks none the worse of sinners whatsoever their deeds, deeming them alone to be seeking happiness in a mistaken way.

And charitable are they who chancing on their wanderings to meet a sick and needy one, send out towards him a thought of health and love; for great is the power of love-charged thought; and laudable is the secrecy of such an act.

O my belovèd, learn to feed other minds with the food of thy love-thoughts; for greatly canst thou benefit them, as also thyself.

Not alone to thy next of kin but to the whole world canst thou be charitable with thy love-thoughts; for to Love is there no obstacle in space, be it ever so vast.

Therefore does the truly charitable one say continuously in his own heart: "Peace be with all beings."

Near to me are those who strive to gain wisdom and knowledge that they may give the same unto others; but alas for those who strive to gain them for themselves alone, for in them the spirit of charity is lacking most lamentably.

Once did a disciple say: *God loveth a cheerful giver,* yet around me do I see followers who make it a merit to feel *pain* in giving; and this they call a laudable sacrifice.

But unto thee I say, joyful is true sacrifice; for the mother of true sacrifice is a joyful Love, and he who makes that true sacrifice understands the real and joyful charity.

Yet only a few there are who understand that real charity—for too many of my followers give alms, but indulge in all manner of evil gossipings and unkindly thoughts towards their neighbours and towards sinners; so do they bestow alms with their hands yet all uncharitableness with their tongues.

But unto thee I say, true charity is one with perfect tolerance for all customs, all beliefs, all weaknesses, all sins; and he who possesses this, possesses Peace in his soul.

OF KILLING AND THOSE WHO KILL

And the Radiant One led me into a beautiful wood, melodious with the songs of many birds, And as we wandered among the trees and flowers a man passed us by—and under his arm was a gun.

And the Master said:

O my disciple, of Love did I preach, and the joy of a great love; but alas, he who delights in the killing of any living thing for his pleasure hath not experienced that great love; and in his heart hath not blossomed the joyful compassion.

Although no man can destroy Life, for Life is eternal, yet do I bid my disciples not to destroy forms either, for cruelty is incompatible with Love.

Yea, cruelty do I call it; yet has man in this respect become so accustomed thereunto that he forgets it is cruelty at all—so hath his heart become hardened.

A countless variety of pleasures hath he, yet out of all these doth he choose for his plaything that which wounds and destroys.

And stony-hearted men there are who torment my creatures, thinking thereby to gain knowledge; though such ill-gotten knowledge is of meagre worth, and could be acquired in uncruel ways. Oh! my son, a terrible sin it is to seek knowledge through the torturing of innocent creatures.

Alas, in some of those very lands where my name is sung the loudest and my image stands at every street corner, are my compassionate precepts the most unheeded; for indifferent are the people to the sufferings of my mute ones.

"No souls have the animals," do they think and say, "therefore it matters not what we do unto them."

But wrong are their assertions, and based on ignorance and lack of clear-seeing; for truly have the animals souls. And one day, albeit long hence, will they be born into human forms.[1]

Verily I say unto all men; the beasts of the field and the pets of the homestead are our younger brethren in the evolutionary Scheme, therefore should they be the recipients of our love and compassion.

[1] It has been given out that the dog, the cat, the horse and the tame elephant possess reincarnating egos, whereas the other animals have their respective group-souls.

OF MOURNERS AND DEATH

And we came to a place of burial, where sorrowful men and women were laying flowers on graves.

And the Master said:

Ah, my brother, harsh may seem the words, yet grief for those who have passed onward to *more life,* often is it but selfishness in disguise; for do the selfless grieve over the joy of others?

Like a heavy garment, forsooth, is the body, and a burden to many who understand not the laws of health; therefore the more so is the shedding of that garment a blessing, for lighter do they feel and rapturously free.

The virtue of compassion did I always extol; ay, but compassion for the ignorance and unbelief of mourners and for the pain-bearing selfishness of those who mourn.

A great compassion do I now feel for these grief-stricken ones in this place of sorrow, and fain would I whisper to them the consolation of Truth. But, alas, too deeply enveloped in their sadness are they for my words to be heard.

And fain would the spirits of their loved ones say: "Mourn not for us, for our pity for your sorrow doth mar our happiness."

And then to the Master I put a question, and said;

Why didst thou say: "Blessèd are they that mourn, for they shall be comforted?" And He smiled as He answered:

Not of those who selfishly grieve for their loved ones did I speak, but of those who because of sorrow turn to that joy which is *within*. And so are they comforted by that one Comfort which nothing can take away.

And now, my son, this would I say to all men of those nations whose custom it still is to bury the dead: Harmful both to the living and to the departed is burial of lifeless bodies, and much disease hath it caused throughout the centuries. Not enough as yet hath man recourse to purification through fire. As ashes, and not as corruption, should the cast-off garments of the soul be consigned to earth.

I have spoken—for those who have ears to hear.

OF MALEFACTORS AND PUNISHMENTS

And the Radiant One took me to a great prison in which there were hundreds of convicts.

And He said:

O my belovèd, did I ever preach the doctrine of revenge, and did I ever admonish my fellows to torment malefactors? Verily I admonished them to be charitable. But even those who professed my name turned deaf ears to my teachings and set up another name which they call *Justice* in its place—for truly their Justice is often but *revenge* in disguise.

A man who is troubled with a contagious disease is isolated, so that he spread not that disease amongst his fellows, and a man who is insane is confined, so that he do no violence: but merely to confine these unfortunate ones will not effect a cure; truly must they receive treatment in addition at the hands of the healthy, and the sympathetic of heart.

And now, learn that in the eyes of the Divine, the sinners are the morally sick; and alas for those who torment the sick instead of seeking to cure their infirmities; for dire will be the result, both to the tormentors and the tormented.

And so, moral hospitals do I bid my followers erect for the erring sons of God, and not places of torment; for to torment is to render the sickly more sick than already they are, and to rouse in them the lust for revenge.

Too inflexible is the law and too unyielding are the minds of many of its administrators, and too indolent the wills of those in power to set about its reform.

Lo, because one man hath slain his fellow he is condemned to death, such being the law, yet although his was the hand that perpetrated the deed, the will of another may have impelled him to commit that deed; for he was obsessed by an evil spirit.

Long ago when I trod the shores of Galilee did I cast out many evil spirits, but now hath materialism discredited my actions and deemed me the victim of superstition.

Yet well were it if those nations whose law it is to slay the slayer should pause and reflect; for I say unto thee that the spirit of many a murderer doth return and obsess the weak and criminally-minded, inciting them to fresh deeds of crime; ay, in this way doth he seek to avenge himself on the law and the community he deems responsible for his death.

But although I have spoken, man will not heed my words as yet, for even knowledge is oft-times at pains to convince ignorance; nevertheless, the time is near at hand when proof shall be given, as even now it is given to those who are willing to receive.

OF WARRING NATIONS

And the Master led me into a place where lay buried many of the soldiers of many nations who had fallen in the Great Wars:

And He said:

O my son, behold with compassion the calamitous aftermath of wrong thought and the result of national self-seeking and competition, and of separateness and jealousy, and of other grievous transgressions against the Law of Love.

Alas, false values have the nations deified; love of power, love of money, love of vanity; but Love itself and the spirit of Love, this have they ignored.

But who understands the meaning of Love and the depth of what it implies? Verily, mutual help is the child of the spirit of Love, and not seeking for self alone as the nations have sought. Ay, and in this have all of them erred to a greater or lesser degree.

Lo, in my churches men have prayed; *Save and deliver us from the hands of our enemies; abate their pride, assuage their malice, and confound their devices;* but for deliverance from their own pride and their own lack of brotherly love have they not prayed in that one-sided prayer.

Though strong was my censure of self-righteousness, too ready have the nations been to behold the mote in their brothers' eyes, but not ready enough to consider the beam in their own eyes, and so, like quarrelsome children have they uttered vehement words and hurled invectives one at the other.

Mild words and moderate phrases did I bid my disciples employ one to another, seeing that a soft answer turneth away wrath, and woundeth not pride. Yet, alas, still too little do those who call themselves my followers pay heed to my words.

For the attainment and maintenance of true peace would I entreat all my devotees in this wise to pray:

"Let the Divine Light of Wisdom illumine the minds of *all* men;
Let the Divine Light of Love illumine the hearts of *all* men—so that Peace and Goodwill may prevail on earth."

Thus saying, the Master led me away from that Place of Remembrance.

OF PEACEFUL POLICY

And the Shining One said:

For the resolving of discords between the nations there are three ways—so deem the statesmen—there is the way of negotiation, the way of threats, and the way of bloodshed. Yet are the last two naught but disastrous illusions; and how can even the first succeed unless actuated by goodwill on all sides and untainted by lust for power?

Lo, there is a blindness which seeth nothing at all, but there is also a blindness which faileth to see that which stareth men full in the face; and with such a blindness are those afflicted who cannot see that only by working *with* instead of *against* can Peace be maintained.

Verily is separateness the real "sin against the Holy Ghost", and it cannot be forgiven, in that forgiveness would be of no avail whatever. Only by ceasing to commit that sin can its evils be prevented.

But maybe thou dost ask: How is it possible

to work *with*, when men and nations so greatly differ in kind and race and character?

Yet have ye not a saying, "live and let live"? Therefore do I charge all leaders and nations to apply the principle of Unity in Diversity, *that* being the Law of God and His Universe. Yea, because rebellious Man in his blindness hath disobeyed that Law of Love, hath he brought about his own undoing.

Self-seekers have the nations been, taking no thought for the good of the world and *all* men.

And power-loving, callous and self-glorifying Rulers have arisen, who lied to and deluded their own peoples, saying: "on all sides are we encompassed by enemies who seek to destroy us, therefore must we be prepared to strike the first blow".

And others have declared: "our peoples grow in numbers and we lack essential materials"—so have they found a pretext for wars.

But this would I say unto all: Why think ye that money was included in the Divine Scheme? Truly not that the love thereof should be the root of all evil, but that it should be used in the right way and at the right time, yea as a power for Peace.

For peaceful commerce was money created, and verily the way of purchase is a millionfold less costly than the way of war and the way of threats.

Peace do the nations desire? Then let those which *have* be willing to share with those which have *not*,[1] so that the causes of envy and hatred be removed for ever, and therewith the causes of war.

And now I will prophesy again, as I prophesied of old. But this time I will not cry, *Woe, woe unto Jeruslaem*, but Glory be to God when that day shall dawn which shall herald the Great Unity, the United Nations of the World. Then shall Peace reign on earth, and men will look back on their follies and squabbles as now they look back on the follies of barbarians.

And lo, that Day *will* dawn, for the way of Good is mightier than the way of Evil, and must prevail in the end.

Blessèd are they who shall hasten its dawning by right thought, right feeling, right aspiration and right sharing, and very dear will they be to me.

[1] This refers to the sharing of raw materials, the unequal possession of which excites cupidity and resentment.

OF LOVE AND MARRIAGE

And the Radiant One led me into a church where a ceremony of marriage was being performed.

And He said:

Much have the wise reviled me because of the interpretation of the foolish, and too much purblind faith hath man placed in the words of my chroniclers, and too little faith in the spirit of my teachings: and so have many shameful and harmful things come to pass.

Morals and customs—these are unstable and changing, and the morals and customs of one land and of one Age are not those of another; therefore the words that I spake erewhile anent marriage and giving in marriage were not intended as laws to be engraven for all beings and all times.

Because I made concession to a hard-hearted people, saying: *Alone for fornication may a man put away his wife,* shall my followers think I condoned jealousy and would have no man *forgive* his wife for bodily unfaithfulness? Verily dearer to me is that husband who forgives his wife and so carries out the spirit of my teachings.

Alas, countless times have my utterances been made a plea for the dissolving of wedlock and for conjugal uncharitableness; and conversely have they been made a plea for the mutual immurement of the ill-matched.

Yet did I ever preach cruelty and the torture of my children? Lo, I say unto thee, those who refuse to unbind the cords of wedlock where two are joined together in misery and mutual repugnance, verily are they torturers in my name.

Yet also do I say unto thee: blessèd are those wedded ones, who having ceased to love one another, strive to love one another afresh, for they are as heroes in my sight and very near to the Father of all Love.

OF HEALERS AND THE HEALING ARTS

And we entered a large hospital wherein were lying many sick and suffering people.

And the Compassionate One said:

A noble and sacred avocation is that of healing the sick, and dear to me are those who pursue it with true sincerity of purpose, and with a deep compassion for their fellows.

Many selfless, high-souled and loving physicians there are, but also many, alas, who have more regard for themselves and their purses and their own repute than for the welfare of their patients.

Hard words, admittedly, are these, yet many sufferers, to their cost, have found them to be true, whilst others will deny their truth, having fared well in the hands of their skilful doctors—thus are they true and untrue.

Nevertheless, countless sick persons are doomed to suffer, seeing that instead of the divine principle of unity in diversity, the sin of separateness prevaileth even in the healing arts. For do not the members of one Group maintain or pretend that they alone are the custodians of truth, and that they alone possess the only right means for the curing of human afflictions? And out of envy, conceit, or ignorance, prejudice or fear, do they not arrogantly denounce all other Groups as either negligible, crankish, fraudulent or dangerous, wilfully forgetting that they themselves have often wrought much harm, and failed to cure where others have succeeded?

Rightly said it is that in all vocations are frauds and knaves to be found, but an unworthy thing it is to make the false a pretext for condemning the true.

Divers methods have the Forces of Good inspired for the healing of human ills, and not rivals are they, but complements one of the other. A proportion of truth and value there is in each of them, yet not the whole truth in any *one* of them; therefore should there be no pride of knowledge, but learning, giving and receiving on all sides.

Yea, too much pride of knowledge and self-seeking obtains where the healing arts are concerned, and because of financial greed and threats to combined-interests do I often see callousness and chicanery, instead of compassion for suffering mankind.

Even shameful conspiracies there are to withhold the truth from the multitudes, and so prevent cures for the most agonizing diseases from becoming known and acclaimed. Thus, those intuitive or skilful men who, because of their valuable discoveries, should be hailed as benefactors of the race, are often reviled as rogues and impostors, and their discoveries denounced as worthless, harmful, or at best unworthy of investigation.

And yet when discoverers are not the unwitting foes of combined-interests, then are they oft times hailed as men of genius.

And so hath it been, and so will it continue to be until love of one's neighbour supplanteth love of self.

Through Love it was that I wrought my miracles when I trod the earth of Palestine—though miracles they were wrongly called.

But as I foretold of yore, such miracles can and are being performed to-day through Love alone; for Love is the true healer.

And let this be marked and inwardly digested: Not through the will, but through the pouring-forth of Divine Love on to the patient, can diseases be cured.

F

OF RE-BIRTH

And as we still wandered we came to a cottage before which sat an old man, and on his knee was a Bible in which he was reading intently.

And the Master said with a smile:

Knowest thou of what that agèd devotee of mine doth read at the moment? Of the Law of Re-birth, though he comprehends it not.

Yet, O my brother, when long ago I walked the shores of Galilee, I taught the doctrine of Re-birth, as also that of Cause and Effect; but as time passed, ignorance prevailed over knowledge, and so did many valuable truths become lost.

And because of this, some of the more reflecting have reviled my teachings and pronounced them cruel and unjust; and verily cruel and unjust they are as many of my followers have represented them to mankind.

Behold these reflecting ones say: "One man is born in a hovel amidst vice and degradation, and another is born in a palace amidst learning and enlightenment, and very difficult it is for the former to acquire virtue in the space of threescore years and ten, but comparatively easy is it for the latter. Thus is the one, having failed, doomed to perdition, while the other attains to salvation."

And so, my Disciple, without the Law of Re-birth and the Law of Cause and Effect or Sequence and Consequence, verily were my teachings unjust. Yet the latter did I teach with emphasis, and the former did I teach also.

Did I not say of John the Baptist: *If ye are willing to receive it, this is Elias, which was to come?* And to Nicodemus I said: *Unless a man be born again he cannot see the Kingdom of God;* yet, alas, have my ministers failed to exercise discernment, so that those things which I meant literally have they taken figuratively, and those which I meant figuratively have they taken literally: thus have confusion and folly arisen.

And now, O my devotee, teach unto thy fellows the truth of Re-birth and the Law of Sequence and Consequence; for know that until man has attained to salvation through the acquisition of the true virtue, he must be re-born again and again: but having attained verily he is made *a pillar in the temple of God, and he shall go out no more.*[1]

And learn also that he who is born in a hovel amidst vice and degradation, is born thus alone because of the Law; for truly doth he reap what once he hath sown.

Why thinkest thou I said unto the man I healed at Bethesda's pool, *Sin no more lest a worse thing befall thee*? Verily because he that sows evil and suffering reaps evil and suffering as the result.

But know this also, that he who sows good, and sows Love and Joy and Wisdom, shall reap all these in return.

And now, to those who already accept the doctrine of Re-birth would I say: Be wise in your knowledge and walk according to your wisdom.

To what end have ye, my loved ones, been re-born? Not alone for the payment of past debts, but for the learning of new lessons and for the acquisition of greater spiritual awareness.

But first shall ye become aware of the lesson which your soul would have ye learn, and to this purpose must ye listen to its still small voice.

[1] Quoting St. Paul.

Too much harking back to the ways and thoughts and habits of previous lives doth prevail among ye, so that one life becomes but an echo of that which went before.

Yea, many of those who walked erewhile along the path of isolation seek again to walk that path, shunning the world instead of profiting by what the world hath to teach.

Or others again lament in their hearts, saying: "In my former life was I free to manifest my powers or my talents, but lo, in this one I am surrounded by barriers."

Yet to them would I say: Even through the valley of limitations shall the steadfast of purpose climb to the summits of Perfection.

And then to the Master I put a question.

And I said:

Master, tell me, why was man not made perfect from the beginning, seeing it is said, God made man after His own Image?

And the Radiant One smiled as He answered:

Without Free-will were Perfection imperfection, yet where there is Free-will there is also the choice between that which brings pain and that which brings peace. Thus may man choose between good and evil.

Nevertheless, the Real Man is made after

God's own Image, for that Real Man is one with *the Spirit of God which dwelleth in you.* And lo! Never was he not and never shall he be *not.*

So saying the Radiant One, after looking very lovingly upon that old man who was still reading the Holy Writ, led me swiftly back to the place of my dwelling.

PART II

My soul was a veritable target for the spears of baneful thoughts that were hurled at Me.

Several years went by; and although while out of my body at night I often visited the Master's garden, and often did He speak to me, nothing further did He give me to set down. And then at last He said: "To what thou hast already written shall be added yet more—for the enlightenment and protection of my loved ones".

And He said:

My ministers in their unknowing have asserted: "In the religion of Christ there are no secret doctrines"; yet did I teach to my disciples many things that I revealed not to the profane and those unqualified to receive them.

For in all religions there is that which is secret and that which is revealed, as the erudite know without the telling. But what is held secret in one age may be revealed in another; and because of this shalt thou among others in these latter days write down the truths it shall be given thee to write.

What say the learnèd of my Gospels? Lo, that they were written long years after my feet had ceased to walk the highways and byways of Palestine. And they speak truth.

And they say also that my scriptures are replete with utterances and doctrines from older religions, from Judaism, from the religions of Egypt, from the religions of Greece and from those of India: and again they speak truth. Yet have the uninitiated made false deductions, so that sceptism has come into being in place of knowledge.

For some have said, "since the religion of Christ is a composite religion culled from many sources, therefore is it a fabrication or the result of fortuitous circumstances". And others have said, it is the outcome of manifold superstitions, and the engrafting of those superstitions upon the story of my life, which they opine, was the story of a social reformer with the fire of fanaticism in his blood.

And even those who do not discredit me and my teachings have been puzzled in their minds as to whether I was not born fivescore years prior to the date of my reputed birth.

And again others have pronounced my life-story, as set down in the Gospels, to be for the most part an allegory portraying in narrative form the Way of Initiation which is the great pathway to God-Consciousness, which in those Gospels is termed the Kingdom of Heaven.

So have the sceptical negated, and the learnèd pondered, and the seers pronounced; yet ever does my life present a mystery baffling to the brains of men.

And inevitably so; for enemies of various sects encompassed me on every side, and because my soul was as a veritable target for the spears of baneful thoughts that were hurled at me by mine adversaries, too intent was I on confounding them to take measures that my deeds be rightly chronicled and my sayings be written down.

Nevertheless, when my days among men drew towards their close, a few of my acts and sayings were truthfully recorded. But the records themselves, because of the persecution of my followers, had perforce later on to be hidden away in a secret place: and only at the appointed time shall they again be brought to light.

But that time is not yet; and even when those scripts shall be found for the puzzling-over by savants, no great satisfaction will they yield save to those who have the key to their hidden meanings.

OF THE SECRET TEACHINGS

And the Master said:

To my first disciples did I teach the eternal verities, and instructed them in the way of Realization and the finding of the mystic Christ. And I taught them of the true nature of man, and of his subtler bodies and of the inner worlds; and of the doctrine of Re-birth, and of Cause and Effect, or Sequence and Consequence, and of other truths and sacred doctrines given only to the chosen and the few.

And after I had passed from their midst, my disciples taught others those same doctrines, so that each generation of initiates instructed the next, as decade followed decade. And these initiates wrought good works and communed with initiates of other schools, and revealed more of those doctrines which had hitherto been secret, so that the minds of the nescient should be enlightened, and men should know that Religion was a science and not merely a belief.

But while the lovers of truth sowed the

seeds of Divine Wisdom which sprang up and blossomed into beautiful flowers, the enemies of Truth sowed noisome tares which choked those beautiful flowers with the evil growths of greed and cruelty and superstition; and lo, what erewhile had been a garden became as a wilderness; for the flowers of Truth were overgrown and hidden by ugly weeds.

Ah, great indeed was the persecution of my spiritual progeny by the enemies of Truth; and many of them perished as the result. Yet the memory of my name did not perish, and as years pursued their onward course, from traditions and hearsay scribes fashioned stories relating of me and my teachings.

And some of these scribes I sought to inspire with the Light of Truth, but oft-times did they obscure it by the clouds of their own imaginings, so that my Gospels became an admixture of verity and falsehood. Moreover, those inner teachings which I had given to my disciples anent the means and the way to Realization were either omitted or so distorted as to be of no avail.

So did my religion become, as it were, a casket with windows of glass through which many precious jewels might be seen but never obtained, for the key thereof had been hidden away: until finally it came to fulfil alone the needs of the simple-minded and the young of soul and the trusting of heart; while the erudite and the more agèd of soul did perforce turn elsewhere in their search for Truth.

OF THE BRIDGE THAT WAS NEVER BUILT

And the Master said:

Lo, the Great Ones ordained that the peoples of the West should learn through the doing of deeds and through the way of action, and the peoples of the East should learn through the way of contemplation and the stilling of the mind: and to teach the felicitous union of these two ways was I born in Palestine; for the way of action is not incompatible with the way of spiritual attainment.

For all things is there a time; for the building of bridges in the outer world, and for the building of bridges in the inner worlds; for the nurturing of the temporal body and for the nuturing of the spiritual bodies which are veritably as the bridge from man unto God.

Yet although I laid the foundation-stone of that bridge for the Western world, the builders that might have been, turned from it away, and the plans of the architect were rejected for those of earthly palaces and great halls in which the worldly did eat and drink and sport and make merry.

Work, performed in the spirit of service to God and to one's fellows, was the ideal I sought to implant in the hearts of the peoples of the West; but too intent on service to themselves were they, and so much under the sway of their worldly passions and desires, that, whilst they prayed to me and sang praises to God, they used my name—as history doth relate—as a plea for all sorts of iniquities. Thus, unknowingly, were they as tools in the hands of mine adversaries.

OF MINE ENEMIES

And the Master said:

In my Gospel it is written: *Those who are not for me are against me.* Yet there are those who are for and against me at one and the same time; and these, forsooth, are my most formidable adversaries, and have been my most formidable adversaries for many scores of generations.

Love of Power is the mainspring of their persecutions, and arrogance and spiritual greed; for from the very beginning of their history have they said amongst themselves: "Lo, it is for *us* to be the custodians of Knowledge."

So did they give out to an all too credulous people that they alone held the golden keys to Truth; and that the age-old doctrines of all previous religions and philosophies and faiths had been inspired by Satan as snares for the entrapping of the unwary.

And threats did they employ, fabricating the dogma of eternal damnation in flaming fires, in place of the just and merciful doctrines of Re-birth and Cause and Effect, as taught by me to my disciples.

Too much of hopefulness did these doctrines engender in the heart of man; venues of escape were they from the clutches of those who arrogated to themselves the sole right to decree whose soul should survive, and whose should perish.

Thus did they prey upon the fears of the trusting and ignorant, having first extolled ignorance as a virtue to be practised in my name.

"Verily, not difficult is it to save the souls of the ignorant," did they opine; "therefore let us make war against learning, that our reward be the greater in heaven."

Ah, truly adepts were they in the art of self-deceiving and self-excusing, and in the fashioning of grandiloquent phrases of self-justification.

Into a fraternity did these lusters after Power form themselves, ay, into a brotherhood for the destruction of brotherhood.

And in that fraternity did they form yet another fraternity—a secret one—so secret, forsooth, that even many of the brothers of the outer fraternity knew nothing thereof, and know nothing thereof unto this day, though still is it mighty for the doing of evil.

And the members of that fraternity insinuated themselves into palaces and high places, and swayed the minds of monarchs and rulers and of those in authority.

Plottings and intrigue did they love, and the troubled eddies of politics which they sought to poison with the poison of their deadly machinations.

For to one end did they labour in their lust for Power—verily to the complete subjugation of the peoples of the West. Ay, dominion over all these did they desire, and lo, they took my name in vain to bring their desire to fulfilment.

Yea, even in this age of knowledge and enlightenment and reason and scientific invention do mine enemies thrive and work in secret, persecuting my loved ones for the attainment of their own ambitions.

And in divers ways do they work, sending spies hither and thither, armed with weapons of falsehood and cunning and dissembling and mendacity, for ever deeming that the end justifies the means.

Where there are those who seek to serve their fellows and to form communities for the dissemination of knowledge or political ideals, lo, do mine enemies work to destroy those communities or bring them into disrepute.

And if they are powerless to destroy them from without, then do they seek to destroy them from within by feigning to work for the same ends, whilst in truth sowing seeds of dissension and strife.

Thus, O belovèd, do they work together for evil, pretending it be for good. And the elder brothers in iniquity sacrifice the younger brothers who are less learned in evil than themselves.

Yet to thee and to all do I say: As the Sabbath was made for man and not man for the Sabbath, so are religions made for man and not man for religions.

And what I say of religions do I say likewise of religious organizations, and the maintenance thereof.

Not for its own sake shall an organization exist, but alone for the helping of man.

OF THE WORKINGS OF MINE ADVERSARIES

And the Master said:

O my belovèd, hard words have I spoken, and these sound strangely on the lips of the very loving, yet even hard words may be as the music of Love.

More hard words have I yet to speak for the enlightening and protection of my children; for like venomous serpents mine adversaries conceal themselves in the grass for their harming or destruction.

And yet he who loves his enemies as I love mine shall be unharmed by his enemies, seeing that Love is the most protective of all shields.

Yea, because those communities which sought to serve me, albeit blindly, along new ways, had not perfected themselves in neighbourly love, so did mine adversaries gain entry into their midst.

For alas, even among my pioneers have I found too much of envy and felinity and unchastity and evil gossipings, so that even these who served me with their right hand oft-times served mine adversaries with their left.

Therefore shall man perfect himself in Love. Yet because the armour of Love is more invulnerable when reinforced by Knowledge, so shall he be given yet more Knowledge.

A long way back into the Past must thou travel with me, O my belovcd, if thou woulds't behold the secret workings of my foes, and behind the Great Veil must thou also look.

As there are currents pertaining to air in the physical welkin, so are there etheric currents pertaining to thought in the spiritual welkin; and the Initiates of the Arcane Wisdom have the power to control these currents and make them subservient to beneficent ends.

In bygone days when my convert, Saul of Tarsus[1], walked among men, did he utilize some of these thought-currents to quicken the minds of the peoples of the West.

But in later days my foes, in their lust for Power, gained ascendency over those cur-

[1] Now a Brother of the Great White Lodge, known as Master Hilarion.

rents, perverting them to serve evil ends instead of good.

Master-minds had those my enemies, and mightily trained in the arts of thought-control and self-discipline were they; and mighty were they also in arcane lore, knowing that forces which had once been apportioned to the cause of Christendom *could not be chained nor destroyed.*

Yea, because the energies of the peoples of the West were given over to the gratification of animal desires and the doing of deeds, rather than to inward-turning and the training of the mind, so did they become an easy prey for mine adversaries and their secret manipulations.

For he who has not disciplined his own mind has formed, as it were, no shield to withstand the attacks of other minds: nay, he wists not even that he is being attacked. Defenceless are the etheric centres in his subtler body, for of their very existence is he unaware, as of the powers whereby they may be controlled.

And of this ignorance did mine enemies have knowledge, taking advantage thereof. Thus were the thoughts and volitions and emotions of men as clay in their hands, to be moulded in whatsoever way they willed.

Magicians were they, skilled in the arts of hypnotism and suggestion and the casting of spells over the unsuspecting.

And not only religious communities and the members of religious communities did they seek to control, but over statesmen and men of learning and men of science did they cast their insidious spells.

And sometimes they worked alone, but oftentimes they worked in a body, assailing their victims from afar with the concentrated force of their attack.

Untiring were they in their will to break down resistance and to lure the steadfast from the honourable pursuit of Truth.

And when they were impotent to achieve their desires, like revengeful children they resorted to tricks and devices and pettinesses, calculated to harass and annoy.

And lo, what they did in days of yore, their descendants in iniquity continue to do now: for mine enemies are not dead.

Look, O my son, behind the veil, and behold them in all their moral nakedness.

Though their garments bear the insignia

of the Religion of Christ, from their throats doth issue a poisonous breath.[1]

As the holy men and ascetics of yore breathed on the sick to render them whole, do these my foes breathe on the sick to render them more sick.

Yet do they appear as holy men and ascetics in the eyes of the undiscerning, for rigorously do they conform to the vows of their calling.

Chaste are they—ay, irreproachable—after the notions of men: yet even their chastity they wield as a force for the making of others unchaste.

Into mind-force do they transform the sex-force: but unto what end? For the augmenting of the moral weaknesses of their victims, and for the weakening of their moral strength.

Lovers of the *One Religion* and the *One Truth* do they proclaim themselves, yet when others preach the *One Truth* in a slightly differing guise, then behold them seated in a body projecting their thought-missiles of destruction.

[1] *Note for Occultists.*—Symbolical of the force which can be projected from the throat-centre of a certain type of magician. Just as a singer acquires vocal control, so do these magicians acquire power in the throat-centre by controlling their own emotions and desires in order to influence the emotions and desires of others.

Leaders do they attack, founders of new communities with ideals of greater tolerance and a greater spirit of brotherhood.

Yea, and even if those communities offer up their love and their service to me with the chants and the ceremonial magic of Christendom, even so do they work to accomplish their downfall by bringing them into obloquy.

Indeed, the very similitude of that magic maketh easier their task, for the laws of Magic are ever based on the rapport set up between like and like.

With powerful words have they denounced magic, terming it sorcery and the black art—which verily it is, when used for evil ends.

Yet are they more culpable than sorcerers; for the sorcerers practised sorcery in the name of the devil, but mine enemies practice sorcery in the name of God.

Pity them, my brother, as I pity them: for many of them know not what they do; and because God is not mocked, their day of reckoning is not far hence.

OF THE COMBATING OF MINE ADVERSARIES

And the Radiant One said:

O beloved, my ways and the ways of the Great White Brotherhood are not the ways of the world, and still less those of mine adversaries: for to me and my Brothers the end justifieth not the means.

With good do we seek to combat evil; with nobler ideals do we seek to fill the hearts of men, and their minds with greater knowledge and power.

Because mine enemies usurped the right to ordain after what manner God should be worshipped, lo, from among the nations we recruited men and women of courage and fortitude who *protested* against this iniquity, and resolved that they and others should worship God according to the dictates of their own hearts.

Protestants were these named, as thou dost know without the telling; for not only did they protest against the spiritual enslavement of their fellows, but also against the greed and evil-doings and licentiousness of those who carried out their enslavers' behests.[1]

Alas, how many perished by reason of their courage; yet did they suffer martyrdom in a great cause.

For the cause of freedom did they die, and not for the substantiation of some theological dogma, though mine enemies would fain have had them believe they were adversaries of Truth.

Thus in many countries did we inspire leaders and preachers whose minds and bodies were strong as fortresses, against which my foes hurled their missiles in vain.

And because the strength of men united is greater than that of isolated individuals, so did the ever-growing body of Protestants become an army too formidable to be routed by my foes.

Yet even the good that my army of Protestants wrought was all too soon to be tarnished with evil.

[1] Those who are conversant with European history of the period need hardly be reminded of the deplorable state of morals which prevailed among priests and prelates, especially in Italy.

Because they did not abide by my commandments and failed to apply the spirit of my teachings and the principle of brotherly love, lo, that one big army split into a thousand little armies, each claiming to be the sole repository of Truth.

Thus even in the vast expanses of Freedom there sprouted the choking tares of bigotry and intolerance with their inevitable consequences, wranglings, revilings and mutual hate.

Nevertheless, the good that had been done could not be undone. But although mine enemies had lost one mighty battle, they had not been destroyed.

Verily not ended was the great campaign, and not ended will it be until to man be given that knowledge of the means whereby he shall behold mine enemies face to face.

OF SCIENCES AND CULTS

And the Master said:

Specialists at creating and exploiting illusions are mine adversaries, therefore is the true scientist an adversary of mine adversaries, for he draweth inspiration from the plane of Pure Mind and abstract thinking—a plane which is beyond their reach.

Not an easy target for their poisoned arrows is he who works selflessly in the pursuit of truth, for he is poised too high for their arrows to ascend; hence do they hate him the more, seeing that they are haters of truth.

Admittedly, not infallible is he, and oft are his discoveries merely approximations and stepping-stones to truth, for in each age can only certain facets thereof be brought to light.

Therefore, not too much should be demanded of the men of science, bearing in mind that in every form of specialism are limitations and pitfalls.

Moreover, by inductive logic doth many a scientist arrive at his conclusions, and only safe is inductive logic if the thinker can be sure that he is in possession of all the facts.

Some scientists there are of smaller stature who are both scientific and unscientific, for they brush aside inconvenient facts as frauds or superstitions unworthy of their notice: thus doth the mirror of science become stained with pseudo-scientific negations.

But this would I say; the time is not far hence when man shall know Truth by direct perception, in that above the plane of Mind is the plane of Intuition, from which all knowledge can be *directly* acquired.

Enemies of religion and of me have scientists and scientific thinkers been called by the bigoted and unknowing; yet never can seekers after truth be mine enemies, for verily they are my friends.

Alone those scientists who devise deadly instruments of destruction are mine enemies for they are the enemies of Love.

Yet not so were those bodies of men who called themselves Agnostics and Rationalists, for though they were destroyers of a certain kind, they were none the less searchers after truth, and therefore served me according to their own lights. Sweep away they did the rubbish of many fears and superstitions and false beliefs, thus clearing the ground for something better to be built up.

But although their leaders in their honesty and confessed ignorance declared: *We do not know*, their fanatical followers declared; *We cannot know, and never shall know.* And some of them cried; *There is no soul, and hence no immortality, nay, there is no God save Science itself!*

And thus, because pride and dogmatism ever close the shutters against the light of further knowledge, did it become needful to inspire another movement as a counteractive to their negations.[1]

No longer should man be dependent on the word of those who believed or professed to believe yet had not *seen.* Proof was he to have offered him in place of that non-comprehending *belief* which had erroneously come to be glorified as a virtue.

Ridicule and sneers and slander were the weapons used to combat this new cult; so was it denounced even by my followers as something evil and ungodly, even though it hath

[1] I.e. Spiritualism.

and increasingly doth bring comfort and healing to the sorrowing and bereaved.

Nevertheless, this do I say; in spite of denouncings and jeerings and revilings, this cult will prevail; for the time has now come to span the illusionary gulf between the seen and unseen, so that man should *know* the truth of his immortality.

And that other cult,[1] which is the synthesis of religion and science and philosophy, shall also prevail. Verily neither of these cults is the enemy of my faith; they are its complements and the complement of each other, and the Blessing of God is upon them.

[1] Viz. Occultism, Esotericism, Theosophy.

THE DAY OF RECKONING—A PROPHECY

And the Master said:

Throughout the centuries have the scientists and even the physicians only seen as through a glass darkly, having been for the most part preoccupied with the grosser manifestations of Nature and not with the subtle.

Of man's physical body much hath been learnt, but as yet little is known about his *etheric body* and his other interpenetrating *bodies* save by occultists, whose word is not believed, and yet is so essential to the fuller understanding of health and disease.

Nevertheless, the ways of the occultist and the spiritualist and the scientist are rapidly converging, though the latter may know it not, or prefer not to acknowledge the fact.

Indeed, by their own long and painstaking methods have scientists discovered many truths long years ago proclaimed by initiates of the Arcane Science, but at that time repudiated as false and fanciful.

Yet whereas human beings can lie and be deluded, not so instruments; and the time is not far hence when instruments of such great sensitiveness will be devised, that Nature will be compelled to lay bare yet more of her secrets before the eyes of even the most sceptical.

And by means of these instruments will the experts be enabled to differentiate between the divers rates of vibration in the ether, and come to perceive how they are being utilized for good or evil ends.

And lo, when the hour shall strike, an instrument will be devised[1] so finely attuned and of such surpassing delicacy that the unseen will become the seen, and the unheard the heard.

And certain strata of the inner worlds will it reveal, and the denizens of those worlds—the evil together with the good.

And those who dwell in the outer world yet use the forces of the inner worlds will also be revealed.

Then will the Day of Reckoning be at hand; for, as in a mirror will mine enemies be reflected, singly or assembled together, intent

[1] Doubtless a species of televisor.

for ever on bending the will of men to their own iniquitous ends.

And thus, suddenly, that which for generation after generation has been veiled in darkness shall be brought to light.

And the tidings thereof will be noised abroad in all the chronicles, and man will rise up in his wrath and overthrow his enemies and mine enemies with the concentrated force of his righteous indignation.

Yea, like a mighty bombardment will he direct his thought-power against his age-long oppressors, having in the interim acquired knowledge of the incalculable potency of Thought.

So will at long last that great brotherhood of oppressors be destroyed, and the abuse of the power of thought recoil on each of its progenitors, as also on the organization for which they have sacrificed even their very souls.

OF THE NEW DISPENSATION

And the Master said:

The cycle of the Old Dispensation hath drawn to its close, and lo, the starry sign of the New Dispensation hath begun to rule the heavens.

New influences will it bring in its wake, new currents of force inspiring man to new ideals, new aspirations, and to the treading of new paths.

Yea, already are its powers becoming manifest; and although the laggards may still walk indolently along the way of old superstitions, and old forms, the daring and progressive have hastened their footsteps; for with the long-established and the time-worn have they shown a laudable impatience.

Think not that I mourn because men have grown weary of hearkening for ever to the self-same story and the old words of Power: lo, new words of Power shall be given to man.

And thereby shall the old forms be shattered, and as with consuming flames shall my religion be depured of its follies and iniquities and its grievous obstacles to Truth.

And those who used the old words of Power for their own ends will stand impotent before the new words of Power, and the new signs and symbols which shall also be given to man.[1]

And before the new currents of force will they likewise stand impotent, unable to wield them, for too rarefied will they be and, as it were, at too high an altitude for them to reach.

Because they have loved power and abused it, to them no longer will power be given, but alone to those who have ceased to desire power.

Too many are there still in the outer worlds who have a liking for power even if they wield it not for iniquitous ends, so must they cleanse their souls of this blemish.

Unperceived doth it oft-times lurk in the subconscious mind; and for this reason amongst other reasons did the Masters of Wisdom sanction the evolving of a new Science —the Science of the Subconscious—for this

[1] These new Words of Power, etc., are already being used in the inner worlds by certain Initiates and their pupils; for all things are manifest in the inner worlds before they manifest on this plane.

also is one of the paths to truth pertaining to the New Dispensation.

Working together for Good shall be the watchword of the New Age, and the goal will be the understanding and perfecting of Man himself.

Then will he come to know that *within* is to be found the mirror of all knowledge.

No longer will he turn outwards as heretofore, suffering his emotions and his mind to be tarnished by the dust of phase and fancy, superstition and fear, but slowly will he turn inwards, until pure of heart *he shall see God.*

Then will become manifest on earth that ancient prophecy—ay, that each man shall become his own law-giver.

Through the knowledge of the ever-just Law of Sequence and Consequence will he cease to do evil, exalting himself over his fellows and seeking to impose upon them his own will.

Nay, to those who still linger by the wayside will he proffer his aid, seeking to give them the knowledge and the strength and the vision whereby they may behold God for themselves.

Thus, my belovèd, of the New Dispensation

have I spoken, and of Aquarius, the sign of the man, which shall inspire Humanity for two thousand years.[1]

Lo, with increasing power will this sign influence the earth and the aureole of the earth, repolarizing with each successive generation the bodies of men.

And thus will the prophecy be fulfilled: *Behold, I make all things new* . . . yea, it will be fulfilled by One Who is greater than I.

[1] See *Through the Eyes of the Masters.* Page 59. By David Anrias.

OF THE RETURN OF THE CHRIST

And the Master said:

Brother of mine, in this my last message at the present time, would I speak of the return of that Exalted One, Whose server and mouthpiece I was in the days of my ministry, and with Whom I also will return when the hour shall strike.

And because His mouthpiece I ever seek to be, what I now give thee to write down for the eyes of men, is in truth His Message, although we speak, as it were, with one Voice.

Those who love me look for the day when I shall fulfil my covenant and return to the world of men—and they look not in vain.

Yet for them is it to appoint the hour of my coming, rather than for me: for of what avail were it for the Teacher to set the new lesson ere the learning of the old one hath in a measure been accomplished?

Long, long years hath my religion been running its course, and although some of my loved ones life after life have diligently applied themselves to the task I set, the majority have been content to bask in the sunshine of their own indolence.

Nevertheless, to each shall be given according to his merit—for such is the Law.

Yea, nothing is lost; and those who unfolded through love and sacrifice in the past, and who acquired noble powers through mystical contemplation and mystical effort, shall be given the gift of memory.

Ay, those powers they acquired in solitude or self-imposed isolation shall return to them even though they live in the noise and turmoil of the world.

Augmented shall those powers be; for in the near future will currents of arcane force, flowing from sacred places in Syria and Palestine, be wielded for their vitalization.

Long ago did I bless those secret places to this end, that they might be as sacred springs whence should flow streams for the quickening of those *who hunger and thirst after righteousness.*

Yea, from these sacred places did I send forth my earliest disciples, with the powers of the initiated, to convert the peoples of the West.

And those my disciples instructed their

followers in the art of arcane magnetization, and the knowledge thereof was handed down to their successors.

For I ordained that objects of talismanic value should be concealed in divers places as well-springs of spiritual force whereunto the faithful might come for healing of body or soul in the days when my Religion would be menaced by doubt and disbelief.

Thus did many sacred places come into being throughout the Western world, and have persisted unto this day.[1]

And over each sacred place doth watch a Guardian Angel[2] who is in spiritual at-one-ment with the Great Heart of Esoteric Christianity itself.

Not in Rome, my son, is that heart, as priests and relates assert, but in a region nearby unto Palestine, where it hath ever been since the day of its birth.

Ay, just as the first clarion note of my Religion was sounded in Palestine, so will its overtone vibrate in Palestine when the hour shall strike.

[1] Lourdes is one of these magnetic centres.

[2] A Deva. See *Watchers of the Seven Spheres.* By H. K. Challoner. Routledge.

Lo, the wheel will have come full swing, and completed will be the circle.

Then once more will I come forth from the place of my seclusion, that I may unify the divers forms into which man hath moulded my faith.

And I will purify those forms, separating in them the gold from the dross, and then moulding them afresh; for though the spirit ever remains the same, the form must be adapted to the needs of each new age.

And as man doth learn to withdraw into the secret places of his heart, so will he learn to build each his own stairway unto God, as was ever the way of the mystic.

Then indeed will the Spirit of those teachings, which long ago I sought to bring to earth, in very truth become manifested in the lives of men, and that bitter wrangling as to the letter, which so discordantly hath echoed down the ages, will cease at last.

Thus from the trammels of self-seeking and confusion, of materialism and doubt, will that true Spirit shine forth as the sun from obscuring clouds: and lo, where darkness was, there shall be Light.

AFTERWORD

Since this script was first published some years ago, portions of it have been revised, others omitted, and a certain amount of new material added to the original text. As this may seem strange and puzzling to those persons who happen to have read the first version, a few words of explanation may be called for, and so are here appended.

To spiritualists, theosophists and students of Occultism in general, the nearness of the (normally) unseen worlds to the seen is an accepted fact, as also the existence of those beings whom they respectively call Helpers, Spirit Guides or Masters of The Ancient Wisdom. Incidentally, the Masters Themselves have often said that They prefer to regard Themselves as the "Elder Brothers" of the race, the difference between Them and ordinary humans being merely one of degree (namely of evolution) and not of kind. But in whatever light They in Their modesty choose to see Themselves, the fact remains—

though unknown to the world at large—that They are ever in close touch with humanity, and seek as far as may be possible to inspire the best in science, philosophy, religion and the arts, inclusive of course of the higher types of literature and ideologies. In many cases They at times inspire poets, playwrights, and others, who are quite unconscious of the source of their inspiration, whilst in other cases They convey Their messages to man through one or other of Their disciples or servers, the latter being Their conscious and willing mediums. These messages having once been published in book-form, the reactions to them are observed by the Masters, so that amendments, deletions or additions may be made in a later edition of such books if They see that it is desirable. For instance, certain portions of a book may either make a wrong, very little or no impression at all on the majority of its readers, in which case, they have largely failed to fulfil the Masters' original purpose, and, therefore, are best deleted or differently worded. It must be noted that despite Their much wider vision, the Masters are not omniscient, and have always to contend with man's measure of free-will and its vagaries, which can seldom be accurately foreseen in detail.

But the following question may now arise: If the Religion of Christ failed to fulfil its Founder's original intentions because the Christ-Teachings were perverted, misinterpreted and appropriated to selfish ends, why did The Hierarchy of Masters not take steps centuries ago to prevent or counteract these inordinations? The answer is to be found in the very backward state of the mental and spiritual evolution of mankind in those days, together with the fact that there were not enough servers or disciples of The Hierarchy living in the world to make it possible. Fortunately nowadays conditions in this respect have greatly changed, and there are a large number of disciples and servers, isolated or forming groups in many countries. These groups are not necessarily religious ones, but are composed of men and women of goodwill who are working in one way or another for the betterment of mankind.

Before concluding this Afterword, it may be of interest to add some data, recently given out by the Tibetan Master in regard to certain things which formed no part of the intentions of The Christ and the Initiate Jesus when They inaugurated the Christian Religion.

First, it was never intended that the Old Testament should be incorporated with The Gospels. Whereas, like the *Ramayama* and *The Indian Song Celestial,* The Gospels come under the heading of first-class Scriptures, the Old Testament for the most part is merely second-class Scriptures, and its incorporation into the Christian Religion, with which fundamentally it has nothing to do, can only be regarded as a major misfortune, seeing that the two are not reconcilable. Indeed, the attempt to reconcile them has been responsible for much of that theological juggling and brain-tormenting which has merely made confusion worse confounded.

Secondly, the intolerant attitude towards matters of sex which has prevailed throughout Christendom was at variance with The Christ's intentions. Primarily responsible for this was the propagandist Saul of Tarsus, alias St. Paul, whose Christianism was coloured by his own personality and the lack of tolerance, understanding and far-sightedness in his character.